DREAM AGAIN

Dream Again After the Identity Crisis

Sherronda Ross-Brown
Foreword By: Dr. Apostle Valerie Jackson

Published by
Daughters of Distinction LLC

Dream Again
Published by Daughters of Distinction LLC
Copyright ©2020 by SHERRONDA ROSS-BROWN

All rights reserved. No portion of this book may be reproduced, stored in a retrieval system, or transmitted in any form or by any means – electronic, mechanical, digital, photocopy, recording, scanning or other – except for brief quotations in printed reviews, or articles without prior permission of the publisher.

Printed in the United States of America

Unless otherwise noted, all Scripture quotations are taken from the Holy Bible, New King James Version.

Scripture quotations marked NKJV are from the New King James Version, Copyright ©1982 by Thomas Nelson, a division of HarperCollins Christian Publishing, Inc.

End-of-verse references and book introductions copyright © 2006 by Thomas Nelson. All rights reserved.

DEDICATION

This book is dedicated to those who have suffered in silence and felt like you were not enough. And that you felt like you had no value or purpose to be here. For all the amazing women, who had to fight for their lives this is for you. I hope this book helps you to find solace.

I would love nothing more than to see this book in the hands of women everywhere far a near who have lost their way but yet willing to find themselves on a healing journey through the power of the Holy Spirit.

That can be a great challenge, but it can be done, and achievable. It is certainly worth the attempt. Even several attempts may be necessary.

But take your time in this healing process, do it with the leading of God. For certain, you can be revived! Surely, you can live again!

In loving memory of those who have transitioned that played a role in my life: My mother & father, Ronald D. Ross & Deborah V. Ross; grandmother, Bishop Viola Reynolds; godmother, Beatrice Wootten. And in loving memory of one of my former pastors, Pastor Robert Brunson, Jr

SPECIAL ACKNOWLEDGEMENTS

This book is dedicated to my Daughter, G'Nelle I love you for life, sweetheart. You are truly a gift from above even though, you may not be able to convey your conversations with me like most others, but we have our very own special way of talking to each other. You are my everything my special jewel and my drive to be better and live better. It is all because of you! We went through so much together and God had brought us through.

Love you Sugarette, you will always be your Momma's girl!

And a Special Acknowledgement to my Spouse, Anthony no matter what at the end of the day you been here through the good and the not so goods. Thank you for your patience during the times of my writing and for your support.

Lovingly,
Sherronda

This shout-out goes to my only beloved sister, Marca Ross-Nicholl of Lawrenceville, GA. She has been such a listening ear during this process and been very supportive in everything that I do. I love you so much the bottom of my heart. You have been my strength in more ways than you will ever know. I appreciate all the time, talks, encouragement, and efforts of reaching out that you have been giving me.

To my Nieces: Marche, Sharae, Mayah, and Tyasia and nephews: Dante, Grant Jr. and Great Nephew, Micah, you all are my sunshine on a cloudy day. I pray that your lives be filled with love, joy, peace, and happiness. May the goodness and favor of God be your portions now and forever!

I love you All,
Your Auntie

To my other relatives! I love you and thank you for all for your continual supports!

And lastly, but not least, Special Acknowledgements go out to two of my best friends: Gwen Simms & Sharon Bailey, who have been here with me through the thick and the thin. You ladies have been my greatest motivators. You have pushed me to never give up and I am so forever grateful to have such friends like you.

CONTENTS

Dedication I
Acknowledgments II
Preface III
Foreword IV
Introduction V

CHAPTERS & BIOGRAPHY

Chapter 1 – Where It All Begins	17
Chapter 2 – The Misfit, Early Years, & Development	21
Chapter 3 – The Next Level of Trauma	27
Chapter 4 – She Think She's Ready to Start A Relationship	31
Chapter 5 - Repeated Cycles and Patterns	36
Chapter 6 – Identity Crisis	42
Chapter 7 - The Trip Up & The Aftermath: Where Do I Go From Here?	47
Chapter 8 - Midnight Cry!! Lord Can You Hear Me?	52
Chapter 9 - The Path to Unlocking My Dreams	56
Chapter 10 - I'm Coming Out/ The Comeback	67
Biography	73

PREFACE

Truth be told, I never saw myself living. I lived my life for others and not for myself. I lost my identity and my way because of the guilt and shame of my past. But, one day God said, "Enough my daughter, "You will live and not die and declare the works of the Lord!" God spoke these words to me "I am turning your mess into a message". Which leads me to the writing of this book.

While writing this book there were a ball of emotions and I discovered there were still same area of pain that I had not fully healed from, but I believe by the time I complete it. God would have healed those areas before the release of this book. My desire that every reader receive the love of God and if there is an area of pain or trauma in your life that you will began to find wholeness and find your identity in Christ Jesus. "Whom the Son set free is free indeed".

FOREWORD

It is with great honor that I provide this Foreword for the "Dream Again" autobiography. The first time I met Sherronda Ross-Brown I ministered to her prophetically that she would walk in a Healing Ministry and there were books that would come out of her pain, I watched this "Beautiful Butterfly" transform right before me from a non-confident woman to a beautiful strong anointed Woman of God. What tried to defeat her became a driving force for determination to succeed in doing the Will of God. Sherronda has a true Servant's heart, she is a Powerful Intercessor, and Woman of many strengthens, Sherronda has helped so many that has connected with in her Women's Empowerment Ministry. I have seen her pour out and console many through encouragement and prayer, she is graced for the broken-hearted and mantled with a Servants Heart for people of all walks of life.

As you read Dream Again, you will see just how strong she has become even Afterr so many life obstacles that tried to cause her to feel defeated, isolated, and confused about her true identity. Sherronda Ross-Brown releases very intimate details concerning life changing events of many trauma's that almost caused her to forfeit a life that God created to be a blessing to the masses. It is with great honor and privilege I foreword Dream Again! I believe this book will touch so many lives, I believe this is just one of many books that will be authored by Sherronda Ross-Brown as a Rising Voice for this generation. She has been graced by Abba Daddy Our Father to bring truth and healing to a Wounded Nation.

Great things are in store for her with a great future and destiny. Sherronda Ross-Brown pours out her life of tears and suffering through this very transparent life changing autobiography. I am confident that many who read this book will not only develop a sense of their true identity but will also gain the true strength and encouragement to one day gain their voice to tell their story. I believe Sherronda Ross-Brown will captivate the audience of those that read this book in such a way that it will begin to cause them to look deeper into their own lives particularly those that have experience simulator traumatic experiences by family trauma, sexual abuse, incest, and molestation, as well as rejection, that have been tormenting many and keep them silent for years.

– Apostle, Dr. Valerie Jackson –

INTRODUCTION

Here is a person who always felt she would never have a true voice. Living afraid to speak up about the real issues she faced kept her bound. Fearing that she would be judged by man as to what she really had to say. Being overly concerned of what others would think or say, if she told her story and afraid it would keep her locked in a box. She struggled with her own inner battles which were rejection, abandonment, hurt, depression, anger, lack of confidence, lack of validation, lack of passion, and so much more. One day, she felt the need to have an "If I can touch the hem of His garment encounter with Jesus"; then she could be made whole. As, she embarks on her journey to find that inner peace. She begins to dream of a place; she was longing to be and one to be healed. It has been a long process of peeling back the layers of years of trauma. And now she is ready to tell her truths.

Can you give me a second chance at life? She really needed one. That was me -- I needed a fresh start, but how can I get there screaming inside? God, please tell me why so much pain? God where can I go and who can I get help from? Just show me the way. This was a heart's plea. She had the faith, but just did not know how to get a grip on those feelings. Someway, somehow; she needed to dream and remember from whence her help came from. She wanted and needed a new experience. She wanted things to change and to work out in her favor.

1 | WHERE IT ALL BEGINS

One day in the fall of November 1974, a girl was born to her parents. She was rejected from the womb of her mother, which was unknown to her until later years. Growing up in a large family, but yet feeling alone. How could she say that with so many people in her home? Well, I will begin to tell you how living in a nine-bedroom house with my grandmother, mom, dad, siblings, cousins, and some adoptive children that my grandma help raised; put me in a place of isolation and abandonment. Even occasionally, church members and friends of the family from time to time were taking in as guests. We all were taken care of all under one roof. From the beginning of my conception, I was not wanted and being young and overhearing a conversation that your dad told your mom that He did not want you; can be devasting for any child. However, my mother kept me anyway and my father was a truck driver that was always on the go; never home, mostly on the road. He was on the roadway more than off the road. When he was home, he would barely be home or hung out with his friends in the streets. My mom was a homemaker, and my grandmother was pretty much the support for the family, by way of the support of her churches. As one of the youngest, I felt deprived and sheltered from many things. Out of all the children my grandmother kept me under her wings for some odd reason. I believe she saw purpose in me. Everywhere she went I went. We were made to go to church. We lived and breathed church twenty-four seven. The church was all I knew and without it, I would have been lost. Growing up was so hard for me; because I was teased and bullied early-on and it started in my elementary school days. I got teased at home and by the neighborhood kids for most of my entire years of schooling.

This all came about because of the lifestyle that was implemented on us being raised in a Holy sanctified house is what they called it back in the day. Our family's rules and guidelines were structured. I was brought up with strict rules, and it was a regulated environment because of our Christian beliefs. It was out of our control, we had to do what was told. All the guidelines that were placed on us was not much of a choice of our own. We did not have much of a say so as children and we dared not talk back, nor not do what was asked. I remember growing up was hard, we were not even allowed to wear certain articles of clothing no pants, make up, and certain jewelry. Back then, it was strictly forbidden and considered a sin. It was just not allowed in our home. Can you imagine at age seven to thirteen looking like an old lady in a child's body? Having to wear your grandmother's clothes to church. And going to school looking like an old lady. Now, Afterr reflecting it was quite an embarrassing moment. And on top of that I was dealing with childhood obesity. Can you imagine wearing church mothers' hats to church like you were one of the mothers of the church? "I know, funny right?" You may say, Wow! And get a good laugh now; because that is what I had to endure. Oh yes, that was me! I even look back now and laugh at what I had to endure. So, that alone messed up my image. To train up a child in the way he should go was an understatement. Everywhere my grandmother went I went. Every church she went to for a preaching engagement, I went and often had to sing. She preached across the city and across many various states. I was just a kid made to do it. Never asked if I wanted to do it or if I wanted to go. I was made to walk in her shoes not literally, but to follow in her footsteps. So much so, I was told as I was growing up you act just like a little Bishop Viola Reynolds. To the point where I began to display some of her mannerisms when I got older. My Grandmother had a heart of gold and helped everybody and loved everybody. She was a good Samaritan to so many. I guess that mantle of giving has fallen on me. She was well-known in the community. When people saw me the first thing, they would say you look and act like your Grandma they said it very often. It felt like people expected me to be like her and wanted me to follow in her footsteps. That caused a major flaw in me. A lack of identity had already begun to develop. At one point in my life, I believed that I had to measure up to who she was. Well, just know that I was not her and that I could never fill that role of being who she was. I was told by different ones in her church to never forget my upbringing or never forget where I come from. Everyone, I felt expected me to be that one family member to be sold out for Christ-like her. Nevertheless, I had not been nor did I want to be. As the word says, we all fall short of the glory of God. Well as I got older, I began to fall, and many times did I fall. As you will begin to see as we go further into the story of my life.

Let us define identity and also what it means to me, Webster defines identity as: the fact of being who or what a person or thing is. (a) individuality (b) who you are, the way you think about yourself, (c) the way you are viewed by the world, and the characteristics that define you. Did you know that our identity is the way we define ourselves this includes our values, our beliefs, and our personality? It also encompasses the role we play in our society and family. Our memories, and our hopes for the future, as well as our hobbies and interest. Most of these things can of course change. This is an excerpt is taken from (Sheri Jacobson).

Here is a list of 7 factors that show you might not have a stable sense of self. (a person without a sense of identity can instead feel a disconnect -from who they have been, and /or no sense as to who they will become next. Taken from the Harleytherapy.co.uk website:

1. You change with your environment.
2. Relationships mold you.
3. You often have radical shifts in your opinion.
4. You do not like being asked about yourself.
5. Your identity crisis means you get bored easily.
6. Your relationships do not run deep.
7. Deep down you do not trust yourself.

Dream Again After the Identity Crisis

Were you aware that a real identity crisis is when we do not form a proper sense of self as an adolescent? And it results in certain ongoing behaviors throughout our adult life. I also would like to add I believe also your identity is shaped by what you see, hear, and have in your environment as a child as well. The memories that affected you in your childhood can also often shapes out how you react to things and do things in your adulthood. Traumas, abuse, brokenness in relationships can often play a vital role in your identity too.

I am fearfully and wonderfully made… Psalms 139:13-17

What does the bible say about identity?
_____
_____
_____
_____
_____

How do you feel about yourself? _____
_____
_____
_____
_____

Have you felt trapped in your life or have you had a loss sense of identity? If so, how does it make you feel? _____
_____
_____
_____
_____

Help!! Who am I? To thine own self, be True? _____
_____
_____
_____
_____

2 | THE MISFIT, EARLY YEARS, & DEVELOPMENT

My siblings had permission to go places and visit other family member, they spent the night and hung out with family and friends. And I had to stay home I got left behind many times. I created imaginary friends and talked to myself a lot. I cried myself to sleep many days when I was a kid and often felt like a misfit. Even at times as I got older. I still feel like the black sheep of the family. This was some of my internal pains often asking myself, "Why am I here and for what purpose?" Why "I" and Why can't "I" type of questions. To finally open and talk about this openly brings about so many emotions. I still feel the residue of the abandonment and rejection of my family from time to time. Even though it has gotten much better. I never expressed this much of myself till now. I asked myself Afterr all this time why do I want to share this. First, of all the first way to heal is admittance. I previously carried so much bitterness, anger, and frustrations, and I keep myself locked in a box and it felt like I was going to explode. The ticking bomb was waiting to go off. But the only thing that kept me grounding was the foundation of my upbringing. The Spirit of the Lord living inside of me and carrying me through would not let me go but so far down. One thing I knew for sure is that I loved God and He loved me. One thing, I was doing wrong was holding all that internal guilt, shame, and pain within. I caused myself so much grief because I just did not know how to convey how I was feeling. I developed unhealthy feelings, emotions, and unhealthy relationships but it all started as a child. Seeing clearer now that what I had done to myself was not good at all.

Now, that I have become older and coming into more understanding. I learning to counteract the things, thoughts, and feelings in other ways. Bleeding internally for a very long time just like the women with the infirmity in the bible who suffered twelve long years. All I wanted was a touch of God. But all I could see is this fragile torn little girl inside of me bleeding and crying from the inside out. Not being able to see my real worth of who God created me to be. All I could see was my devasting history. Which in turned caused more trauma. I encountered many triggers and many mishaps in my life that lead me into making bad choices throughout my life. It is not like I had an overall bad childhood until other things began to unfold. Always analyzing and questioning myself like what have I done? Why do I have certain behaviors? Why do I feel this way? Why so many repeated cycles, etc.? It got to the point where I did not want to look myself in the mirror. Even though I could not change the things I put myself into or change the things that happened to me. I tried to seek out for healing for the traumas but was often misunderstood. And that kept me in a place of hurt too and kept tripping me up, as well. It is a sad thing when you try to reach out for help, but no one can help you or may not be able to understand your level of pain. I tried to get closure and tried not to think about those things, but it had such a deep grip on me. I went to church, being saved, and all but broken inside. I was saved but needing true deliverance. My past followed me everywhere I went because, I never get properly healed from the abuse of my childhood. What abuse you might ask.

Let us talk about it for a minute, in my early years of around maybe nine or ten, I opened a door of perversion that would affect my life. The first mistake was one of my close relatives and I played house the game of mommy and daddy, you can figure that out. When we were kids, we did not know what we were exactly doing or even knew that it would affect our lives when we get older. Well, at least for me I did not know what I was doing. Late at night, we would sneak in my mothers' room and watch explicit movies on television while my mom was asleep. By watching these shows it began to awaking things in our bodies to explore. And bam the touching began not to become too graphic; you

Dream Again After the Identity Crisis

can imagine what was happening. The spirit of perversion is real and can hit children too. I never knew in a million years the magnitude of the impact it would have on my life. I had no clue what we were doing would create other things to happen to me in my atmosphere in later years to come. I am not sure how long it lasted but not only did that happen. But one of the adoptive boys that my grandmother was caring for was touching me, as well. He was older than I and made me do things I did not want to do. They made me do some perverted things to them and act out what we saw on television. I was gullible and I never stood up for myself nor did I say no or tell anyone about it. So, from elementary to high school this perverse spirit followed me. It got so bad that some of the neighborhood boys used to take advantage of me too, and I kept it all silent. As a result, I became very sexually active and addicted to porn in my teens it carried into my adulthood until I realized I was damaging my life and body. I dealt with a tormenting spirit and it hunted me for years. It may sound weird, but this was my life it was real, and it is nothing funny about it. I can even remember one time when I was a small, one of the males in the church came and stayed over in our home. While there, he touched me too and made me do things to him. That spirit would just follow me as if it knew I would give into their request and out of fear of what they would do to me. It was like they could pick me out of a line-up and says she the one and I would never say, no. It was as if I just invited them to do whatever they wanted me to do. I was always told I better not tell anybody and who would believe me. So, therefore; I keep quiet.

By time I got to high school, I was already ruined emotionally and physically. You may say how did all this take place under such a Christian household; well, it did. Yes, just because I was raised in Christian household Pentecostal/Holiness, to be exact. Let me put this disclaimer out their just because you are raised in a Christian home does not mean the devil does not cause havoc or try to destroy their families too. I believe they go through tremendous warfare, as well. It is just that the public just do not know a lot about what happens in their homes. Being raised in such an environment, does not neglect the fact that things does not happen. And the bad thing about it, is that oftentimes there are hidden secrets. As well as, ancestral and generational curses in the bloodline. Those hidden things are taken to their graves. It does not mean that because you live in a Christian home that things are perfect. It is far from that, especially in mines. It was undercover things in my bloodline, and in my family that no one ever talked about. To be honest, I found out that sexual perversion ran its course in my bloodline through some of my ancestors.

As I got older, I found out there were rapes, incest, homosexuality, and alcoholism in my bloodline. All covered up and not addressed. Until, when a family member passed on; then things came to surface and out of the woodworks. Then, they wanted to bring up past histories of the family members and what happened within the family. Family members went to their graves with hidden secrets. My very maternal grandmother was a product of a rape. Wow, just wow! There was a pattern that I began to recognize as well, in my bloodline many of them dead from cancer and it tried to put fear in me for a while. My mom, and a few aunts, and cousins also died of cancer like what the world is going on in my family. I was like it will not happen to me or my daughter this spirit of death has to cease in Jesus' name.

Can you see why I related myself to the women with an issue of blood? I was sick and felt unclean, but most of all I wanted to have faith enough to know that God could heal me. All I wanted to do is press forward to touch the hem of God's garment; so that He can make me clean and whole. But I knew it was going to require me to go through a process. What should have been a safe atmosphere and safe environment was full of wickedness and deceitful works. What is God intended purpose and plan for the family? The plan and purpose of the family is to prepare every individual for a creative and spirit-filled life and coming to know who we are, which derives from what we are taught, seen, or heard in the family's daily living. And my belief is that we are better when we are in a loving and caring nurturing environment.

2 Chronicles 7:14 speaks regarding that, if a family is humble and call to God, He will heal that home. As parents care, we are admonished to allow revivals in our homes. I admonish every mother to love their daughters and their sons and every father to love their sons and daughters. Show our children genuine love, and validate them, support them, pour into them, and love on them. Never to show favoritism. So, when they get older the things that were taught would stick and carry them into their adulthood and when they get older that legacy will carry on into their next generation.

Prayer for Families:
I pray that every wicked plot and plan against our families and our bloodline will not prosper. And every generational curse is broken off us. That every demonic influence that can infiltrate the family and call rejection and abandonment to cease. I pray that the Love of God is displayed and that we will begin to teach our children Godly principles and keep them shield and safe. That we will cover our children in prayer and even talked to them to see how they feel in their day. I pray there will not be a hidden agenda or hidden things that the children have to hear that would cause them trauma in their adulthood. We close the door of abuse and perversion and that God will cover them in Jesus Mighty Name, Amen.

Add your own personal prayer that you would like to add concerning your family and or your children that needs to be improve or changed.

_____
_____
_____
_____
_____

Matthew 9:20-22 - 20 Just then a woman who had suffered for twelve years with constant bleeding came up behind him. She touched the fringe of his robe,21 for she thought "if I can touch his robe, I will be healed." 22Jesus turned around, and when he saw he said, "Daughter, be encouraged! Your faith has made you well." And the woman was healed at that moment. God wants us whole and healed. We just have to be determined in the press. We need to be honest and release those pains even if it requires seeking help with what we are feeling.

My Gosh, what do you do when your family dynamic is jacked up!

Dream Again After the Identity Crisis

What issues or secrets are you or have you carried that weighing you down that requires you to touch God to obtain your healing? _____
_____
_____
_____
_____

Do you believe that you can be healed by the Power of the Holy Spirit? And if so, what steps are you willing to take to get to your healing?
_____
_____
_____
_____
_____

Did you seek professionally or spiritual counseling to help you cope with your situation why or why not? It is okay to talk to seek help if you need it.
_____
_____
_____
_____
_____

Were you or are you bitter, anger, or hurt? Are you willing to forgive your loved one that may have hurt you be it through rejection, or abandonment? Forgiveness is a major key in your process.
_____
_____
_____
_____
_____

3 | THE NEXT LEVEL OF TRAUMA

The next phase of my life consisted of graduating from high school, getting pregnant, and so forth. As I am approaching my seventeenth birthday, I met a young man in high school we began to talk and enjoy each other company. I would secretly invite him over late night to come to see me while everyone was asleep. He would enter my bedroom handle his business and leave. When we saw each other at school, it was as if nothing ever happened between us. I liked this young man and I thought he liked me too. He gave me attention Afterr hours, but during daylight I was non-existent to him; I was hurt. He even told me he was going to take me to his senior prom. He was a year ahead of me. He promised me things and would always renege. Here, comes my first level of boyfriend rejections and it left me devastated and humiliated. Even Afterr that, I continued to see him off and on for a while. Until my senior year, then I was introduced to another young man by a mutual friend. This young man seemed to have had it somewhat together and was showing interest. I met his family, they appeared to be pleasant, honorable, and seemed like a well-kept family. We began to date and right off the back; we became sexually active. Then bam, I get pregnant at the age of eighteen, the year of my graduation. I found out the month before my senior prom that I was pregnant.

Dream Again After the Identity Crisis

So, moving forward may graduation came and now fast forward I about to go into motherhood. Talking about a shocker. We had started making plans and even talked about getting married. Due to unexpected circumstances, my baby comes earlier than we expected. I was only five months into my pregnancy when I delivered her, I was not ready yet but now having to accept motherhood and having to take care of a premature baby. Lord knows I was not prepared to be a mother yet but, had to grow up fast. My baby was sickly, and the doctors thought she was not gone to survive. She needed me too be strong to help her survive. I stepped up to the plate and did what I had to do. I moved out of my parents' home and moved in with my baby father home and with his parents so they can help me with the baby until I can get on my own feet. My baby girl was only 11 ounces and birth and stayed in the hospital for three and a half months. I was scared as a first-time mom not knowing anything about raising a sick baby. We did not know if she would live or die. Blessed be to God she survived even though she had some hard times to overcome. By the Grace of God, she has overcome a lot of obstacles. We found out a few years later that from her prematurity that she developed cerebral palsy, along with multiple disabilities. I still had the desire to keep her, nourish her, and love her to the best of my ability. I stayed with her father for about two more years until I got a place of my own and tried to gain a sense of independence.

While going through the stress of raising my baby. Her dad decides he cannot handle the pressure and did not want to be in a relationship with me any longer. I had to keep moving forward; because now, a baby was in my life. I went through some highs and lows, went through some rocky moments but had to still keep pushing. On top of that, it gets to the point where the father of my child does not want to have rights to his child anymore just visitation and that was random. In spite of circumstances the Favor of God has always taken care of our need's no matter what. He has always had his hand on my life even when I could not see it. Here, in this phase of my life I started to get the hang of motherhood and had become somewhat stable. I am in my own apartment and running back and forth to doctor appointments and hospitals on a constant basis for many years to help my child develop properly. Once I got stable and was doing good on my own here comes a counterfeit friendship. I met another man one day while walking to

Dream Again After the Identity Crisis

the store. He was fine as sliced bread, so I believed. He was built just the way I would have wanted a man. He pursued me and we dated for almost three years. I got pregnant with my second child with this man. The baby was born early too and did not survive. I had a miscarriage another devasting blow. This young man did not love me either. But I thought he did. We would stay over each other apartments. We had some good and bad times. He was cheating on me with other women during our relationship. I was so over hills for this man that I would try to do anything to hold on to him. He was a little older than I and I felt that is what I needed for my life. He worked and had his own. I thought he was going to be my permanent man. Well, I set my own self up for failure why because I found myself in a place of somewhat always wondering what he was doing, where he was at, and with whom he was with constantly because of the cheating. He would take my car go out and not bring it back for a few days and I would not know where he was. He always had some sort of excuse for why he did not come back, and I fell into the trap of lusting because it was not real love. So there go another level of rejection from a man.

Closing that chapter of my life with him was hard for me to do, but I did it for the sake of moving on. Afterr a period of time of being alone Afterr that ordeal, God began to build me up and started opening doors for me. He begins to transform my life into something better. I began to get to know him again especially as my Savior and my provider. I was not perfect but striving to do better for me and my child. I got a job and was holding it down. Finally, things started looking better for me. By the time, my daughter turns three or four I was doing well, I was working a pretty decent job, I had a car, and God had blessed me with my first-time homebuyer three-bedroom home.

Have you ever experienced an unexpected blow or unplanned situation in your life? If so, how did it make you feel?

_____
_____
_____
_____
_____

Dream Again After the Identity Crisis

Do you have any regrets from your past and have you dealt with them? How do you plan to overcome it if you have any regrets?

_____
_____
_____
_____
_____

Life can cause us to go off the beaten path, in which, God has intended for us. If you gotten off track what steps can, or would you taken to get you back on track?

_____
_____
_____
_____
_____

At times we move to fast in making decisions and not wait on God for what best for our lives. Have you ever found yourself going ahead of God in making decisions for your life? If so, what lessons have you learned about moving ahead of God?

_____
_____
_____
_____
_____

4 | SHE THINK SHE'S READY TO START A RELATIONSHIP

Finally, on my own doing very well for myself and raising my child. Life started to appear good for a moment, Until I think I am ready to move on and start dating again. See! There was something that always made me feel like I needed someone in my life. You will begin to see more of a wanting and needed pattern here that I could not see or recognize. Unhealthy relationships as well as bad behaviors being displayed back-to-back this was a lack of self-worth. I jumped into another relationship and did not give myself time to heal from the others as you can see now how the patterns were formed.

Let us see how some more things unfolded. At my job that God had blessed me with, I met a young man, and we began to date; it lasted a little over two years. He also made me promises that he did not honor or keep. He promised me that we were going get married Afterr dating for nearly two years. He played me like a puppet and guess what? He was already married but living a double life. I was his secret work wife. Everyone at work knew us as a couple and many even knew he was married, but I never knew until later on in the relationship. Once I find out about it, we still saw each other off and on and keep it quiet. This was until, he introduced me to his nephew who came to town to start a new life in Virginia. As I began to talk with his nephew, we hit it off pretty well. I never spoke about the relationship that the uncle

Dream Again After the Identity Crisis

and I had. We never told anyone about the affair and at some point, it stopped. As I began to hang around his nephew more, we began to build a bond, and I believe that was the intent of the uncle for him and I to hit it off so the heat can be taken off of him and that he would no longer be entangled with me. Afterr six months of talking to the nephew, we decided that we wanted to have a life together. But yet I had this secret over my head, and I ended up getting married to him. I was twenty-five years old at the time and he was nineteen. Afterr the wedding, I could not stay in the relationship with this whole lie over my head. I could not stand the pain and my conscience was eating me up inside.

Now, being in a new relationship and freshly married one day my spouse and I were talking, and he asked me a question about his uncle. He kindly asks me if anything had happened with the uncle and I and He said he felt like something had happened between us; because of the way he used to look at me and the way he would speak to me, but he just could not put his hands on what it was. So, I confessed to him. Once the truth came out, he still accepted me, and our lives went on as usual. However, Afterr a year and a half of being married, he gets homesick and wants to move back to his hometown of Kentucky. He was a momma's boy and anything she said pretty much he went with. He decides to leave me and go back home for a length of time Afterr I had just finished paying off a debt of $10,000 of wedding expenses, along with paying on a mortgage on a brand-new house. I was left to pay those debts by myself, but I got through it because I had a decent job at the time.

Right Afterrwards, things start happening a down spiral one thing started happening Afterr the next. My child began to develop seizures and became very ill. back-to-back hospital visits again. And here I am just trying to work and stay afloat, but something had to give. So, I took a leave of absence from my job to take care of her that was top priority. So, I took the family medical leave it secured my job, but I had no steady income coming in. Therefore, it caused me to get further and further behind to the point I could not catch up anymore. I filed bankruptcy thinking it would buy me some time and tried to save my house. The lenders would not let me keep the house; because I had not been it long enough, so I had to move. Once again devasted, because

Dream Again After the Identity Crisis

it was my first home that God had blessed me with before I had even gotten married. God had opened a door for me, and I allowed my own fleshly desires to cause me to lose what He had given me. I took his blessings for granted. While going through that process of losing the house, the spouse decides he will come back home to try to help me, but it was just too late. The house was already being taken from me. So, we decided since I lost the house that I had nothing left here other than my job keeping me in Virginia. We decided to relocate to his hometown of Kentucky, and I gave up my life here to get a fresh start.

Now, I am in an unfamiliar place and do not know anybody. I felt like I was living in hell or a nightmare what I had to endure was overwhelming. His family put me through some rough times. I tried my best to get through it. God opened some doors for me while I was there. I got a job and was able to get an apartment. I moved out of his family home. I thought once I was able to get on my feet things would improve. Well, that was not quite the case, things got worse before they got better. I was the only one working; I was not even out there a good year, when this so-called spouse starts tripping out and begins to display things that I never ever saw him do before, while he was here in Virginia. He seemed like such a gentleman when he lived in Virginia with me. But my goodness, I was fooled. He showed me some excessive damaging behaviors that I never knew he even had in him. All kinds of craziness began to happen. I was being accused of things that I was not doing and had not done. I met a couple that knew him and his family and was finding out that they were reporting stuff to him. And telling his family things that I was supposedly was doing or not doing etc. I was lied on; I was accused of cheating on him with his friends which was a lie. I actually was faithful and committed to the marriage. Being talked about, mistreated, stolen from, and was even told by someone in his family that they hoped me, and my child would die; affected me psychologically. So much happened to me, number one, because I was disobedient and hard-headed.

Secondly, I entered a marriage that God did not ordain but in all that God still brought me through. I never lost my faith in God because, it was him that always sustained me and kept me. I found a nice church and met some awesome people who supported me during my time of living there. To this day, I still have contact with that family, and

Dream Again After the Identity Crisis

they embrace me as one of their extended children. Without them, I probably would not have made it as far as I did out there. I stayed in Kentucky for eight long years until I got sick and had an emergency surgery and then I realized that I was alone and had no family to help me and nobody would be there for me and my daughter, if something should have happened to me. So, I began to search for ways to come home which led to the next level of misfortunes in my life.

At times we move to fast in making decisions and not waiting on God for what best for our lives.
Have you ever found yourself going ahead of God in making decisions for your life? If you so what lessons have you learned about moving ahead of God's.

_____
_____
_____
_____
_____

Do you realize that disobedience surely brings about consequences?
_____
_____
_____
_____

Have you move out of God's timing before in your life"? what was your experience?
_____
_____
_____
_____

Dream Again After the Identity Crisis

You surely reap what you sow it may not come the way you created it but it surely going be something you have to reap. What is an area of disobedience you need to work on? If God says no are you going tell him yes anyway?

_____
_____
_____
_____
_____

5 | REPEATED CYCLES & PATTERNS

In 2003, I met a male on a dating website. I was once addicted to the chatrooms that AOL once had back in the day. It became my best friend. It was a place where you can meet and greet people based on a certain category that you searched for. This man that I met, we had been talking on and off for a period of time and was getting to know each other more than online dating. I found out that he lived in Virginia and not far from my hometown. It was Christmas season and he asked me what I wanted for Christmas. I told him I wanted to come back home, but I did not know how I would get back there. On December 24, 2003. He drove to Kentucky a thirteen-hour drive to come get me. I left with him me and my baby. All I took was our clothes and we drove all night back to Virginia. Now, granted I really did not know much about this man other than what he shared with me by phone and online. He could have been a serial killer or something I just left and went with him. All I knew was I wanted to come back to Virginia, not necessarily wanted to come back to Richmond, but at least near home. I moved in with him and we resided in Northern, Virginia. I was hoping that we could start a relationship so I could forget about the past that I left in Kentucky. Before I even left Kentucky, I had filed for my divorce and it was granted in that same year of my leaving. So, I was free to date or start over if I chose too. This man had talked a good game too. But the true reality is that I could not see the pattern or cycle that I was going on with me. Through these men were bad for me I was

Dream Again After the Identity Crisis

bad for them to cause I had a major problem going on inside of me.

But see that what happens when you do not see the value of your worth and not knowing your identity. You settle and you get comfortable in your own traps. You allow things to happen in your life that not so good for you. You are very weak and become an easy target to be used because you are in a vulnerable state in your life. Let keep going with this misfortune. Afterr a year of living with him I thought we would have a life together and get married someday. At least that was the plan that we talked about. Well, let just say things began to change in this situation. Afterr some time, his attitude began to change towards me, he would become snappy, and be verbally abusive towards me and I was not used to that. He started flipping out on me almost daily. I questioned what in the world is happening? And did I do something that I am not aware of. So, one day unexpectedly; he comes in from work with these folded empty boxes. He never said what they were for or who they were for. Until one day, I asked him. He said, "Well! I thought this is what I wanted -- to be in a relationship with you and that we would someday get married, but I realized I am still in love with my daughter's mother, and he wanted a life with her.

Wow! What a shocker and devastation to my heart all over again. Like, Lord can I get a break! The break should have been me taking a break from myself destructions. I was blinded by my owns desires. He tells me when you ready and can find you somewhere to go to do just that. And because of the way he spoke it and how he handled the situation it made me fearful for my life and my daughter's life. I knew I could not stay in that environment much longer it seemed like the more days I was there they more frustrated and angrier he got. I mustered enough strength to call a domestic violence hotline and I explained to them what had happened, and they asked me was, "I scared of him and afraid to stay in the house with him?" And I told them, Yes! Thank God it there was not any physical altercations, but the mental and verbal abuse was enough for me to leave. Afterr the call, this lady came with a van and got us up out of their and took me to a domestic violence shelter while he was at work. We jetted out of there so that it would not be any conflict or issues. I lived in this shelter for almost two years and my family had no clue where I was, and I never told them that I was there. I did not want my family to worry about me nor did I want them to know what I had done or what caused me to be there. I keep that part of my life private. It had nothing to do with pride. I just did not want to face the reality of my screw ups or be judged by them, so I keep the internal secrets. Feeling like damaged goods and feeling like no one would ever want me Afterr all that or even ever finding true love, my self-esteem was shot. Another broken relationship, yet again, putting my daughter in the middle of all this because of my selfishness and unfilled voids and lack of validations. All I really wanted was to be loved, be in love, and have a family of my own differently from what I felt and had experienced as a child. I was not only hurting me but hurting my child emotionally. She had to see my tears quite a bit and I am sure she felt a sense of pain, even though she could not convey it. There were plenty of days I cried from the despair and heartache of another man hurting me.

In actuality, it was me that was hurting me. You would have thought that I would have learned some lessons and that I would not search anymore and that I would give myself a break from relationships, and hook ups for a while. During my time at this shelter, they help me try to rebuild my womanhood from being fragile and shattered all over again through counseling and educational services it helps me some. In the midst God showed up and I will never forget this moment as long as I live. My daughter was not feeling good and was running a fever. So, I walked down to the street to a service station at the corner from the center to get her some Tylenol and there was a couple just sitting in their car drinking on some coffee minding their own business. And as I stepped out of the store, they spoke to me and ask me how I was doing it was like God had them sitting there just for me. The gentleman asked me did I know Jesus and if I had a personal relationship with him. I replied yes, I know Jesus! And he said are you going to church? I responded, "No, I am new to the area and I do not know anyone here." I told them that I was staying in domestic violence shelter up the street and it was an undisclosed location; so, I could not tell them exactly where it was. And furthermore, I did not have a car to go to church. So, they asked me to sit in their car for a minute to talk to them, so I did. I felt a sense of peace with them for some reason. They offered me a ride to take me to their church and began to explain to me that the church was non-denominational and that they believe in the power of the Holy Spirit to flow and have its way. And because I was

Dream Again After the Identity Crisis

very familiar with that kind of talk. I told them that I would visit if they could pick me up. I would walk to the service station where they would come to pick me up and that how I got back connected to the church. This couple was God sent it was truly a divine connection not only did they introduce me back to Christ, but I became an extension to their family. They loved on me and supported me as if I was a natural-born child. They prayed for me, counseled me, and look out for me while I was in their area. They even helped me find a place to stay in the next phase of my displacement. They made sure wherever we went that we would be in good hands.

Before I left the first domestic violence center to go on to the next location, God started opening doors for me yet again. He has always been with me. No matter how much I screwed up God always led me back to Him. He did not let me go but so far down in anything I did. That the kind of God I serve. He is one that will sustain you and keep you. His word tells us that He will never leave you, nor forsake you. He was just that for me. The shelter blessed me with a car so I could get to point A to point B. It was not a fancy car, but it was transportation, and I was free to travel and did not have to wait for anyone to take me anywhere. With that blessing, I was able to help other ladies in the shelter to get to the store, dr. appts, and help them get to the places they needed if I was able to. I was able to go to church on my own and did not have to walk down the street to the service station anymore to go to church. And when it was time for me to transition to the next center. I had a way to do things that I needed to do to provide for my daughter and me. When I moved to the next homeless shelter, which was called "Serve." Wow, what a name! I never thought about it until now. The name "Serve", it speaks volumes to me why because that exactly who I am and what I have done for years serve others. Being there in this new place was very uncomfortably but valuable lessons needed to be learned during this time of the transition. God had to deal with me on an entirely another level because, all "I could do was be dependent on him for everything concerning my life at that point. During this transition of being at "Serve" God met me in unconventional ways. He would minister to my soul in quietness of the night or He would minister to me by way of a song to keep me in the remembrance of him. He would bring familiar words back to my mind and He always

Dream Again After the Identity Crisis

had a way of letting me know he loved me and was with me no matter what.

When you are in a low place or if you have experienced being in a low place. How did God meet you? _____
_____
_____
_____
_____

Were you able to identify any repeated patterns or cycles in your life that you could not seem to break free from?
_____
_____
_____
_____
_____

Did you seek God as to why and where did those patterns or cycles come from? And whether it came from your childhood, adolescents, or from an unexpected trauma in your life.
_____
_____
_____
_____
_____

Do you feel like a failure because of your repeats? In what way can you make yourself feel better? _____
_____
_____
_____
_____

Dream Again After the Identity Crisis

Here are some comforting Bible verses to encourage you when you feel alone:

- **Deuteronomy 31:8-9** - The Lord himself goes before you and will be with you; he will never leave you nor forsake you. Do not be afraid; do not be discouraged.

- **Psalms 34:18** - The Lord is close to the brokenhearted and saves those who are crushed in spirit.

- **Psalms 147:3** - He Heals the broken hearted and binds up their wounds.

- **Isaiah 41:10** - Fear not, for I am with you, be not dismayed for I am your God; I will strengthen you, I will help you. I will uphold you with my righteous right hand.

Self-Reflective Moment

Now, that we have reflected on some moments in our life. Write down some of your feelings and pray over it making sure there is still no residue of pain in those areas. And if it is asking the Holy Spirit to come in to heal those places in your life that you still struggling in. And if there is a sting or ounce of pain that God would remove it from your life. (Be Free from it today!!) In Jesus Mighty Name!!

_____
_____
_____
_____
_____
_____
_____
_____
_____
_____
_____
_____

6 | IDENTITY CRISIS

I thought I was beginning to rebuild my life at the Women and Children Shelter. They had found me housing in one of their transitional homes. The month that I was supposed to move in, things change once again. My precious child had dislocated her hip which required me to travel back and forth to Richmond to bring her to the Children's Hospital and from there she had to be placed in the hospital to have surgery and to have her recovery time. During this time, I did not have a place to stay in Richmond. Even though I had family, I did not want to put a strain on them or ask for help now that where the pride came in. I did not want to reveal that I was living in a shelter. Therefore, I contacted a male friend that I knew living in Petersburg, VA. He offered me a place where he was staying. He lived in a hotel and gave me access to his room, so that we could be safe, and it would make life a little easier so I would not have to travel back and forth from to Northern Virginia. So, I took him up on his offer, and in the back of my mind, I wanted to see if we could start a relationship. But instead, we lived as roommates with benefits. It was supposed to be temporary until my child recovered and then I would go back to NOVA. But here is the monkey wrench in those plans, her recovery time was longer than expected and she had to stay in the hospital for a little over six months. And because of her length of time in hospital. I lost my placement for my transitional home. The shelter was like they have to give it to someone else cause they could not hold my placement

Dream Again After the Identity Crisis

any longer, which caused me to have to stay in the hotel longer than I wanted to; but I made the best of what I had. While trying to pursue a relationship with this new guy. I found out that He had gotten another young lady pregnant that he was seeing before I came into the picture. He was generous enough to let me stay in the room and he moved in with her and proposed to her. But all the while he would come back and forth to visit me, to check on me all the time.

Now, I am really frustrated at how things are turning out for me disappointment Afterr disappointment. I was just sick of it all at this point and just wanted to give up and die. I was so stressed that I took a bottle of pain pills because I could not take the stress anymore. I just wanted to die. I felt like life was not worth living anymore. I should have been died right now. But God! On this day, the young man came by to visit and found me passed out on the bathroom floor. He called 911 and got me to the hospital. It had to be God. He is a Keeper and He kept me once again. There must have been a greater purpose, even though I could not see it. I could have lost my daughter and she could have been put up in foster care system somewhere, but God spared both of us. During that time, she had already come home from the hospital. However, God spared her life when the police and EMT came I was told that they asked him about her. And asked him about her family, of course, he did not have any of that information about me or her. So, he told them that my child was his and that He would take care of her until I return. He said he fought for me, so my child would not be taken away from me; because he said he felt like it was his fault that I had a breakdown. Afterr I got released from the hospital. I immediately tried to find myself a nearby church to reconnect to God. As I stated before, I have always known where my help came from. Even though, I kept making stupid, senseless, and self-inflicted decisions. I found myself in a very low place all over again. I was truly running from my own self and from the purposes and plans that God had for me. I was just searching all over again for the perfect man to come to my rescue and free me from myself. I met a couple of men and started the dating process once again through online dating services.

In 2005, I met my second husband; we dated for about six months. I moved in with him and within that year we got married. He was looking for companionship, and a soulmate and I wanted the same but

Dream Again After the Identity Crisis

yet my heart was still empty. But also, for me at that time honestly, I just needed stability and better housing conditions. For months things were okay with us. I felt safe and we were growing and learning from each other in the beginning stages of a marriage. But then the problems of incompatibility and control began to manifest. It was constant disagreements, and lack of reasonings. I did not know if I was coming or going. I did not recognize who I was anymore at all. I was under so much control and bondage until I just settled because I did not want to feel like a failure yet again. I lost my identity even more which it was not much there, but it was completely gone now. "I lost my way" However, I stayed in this marriage for two and a half years. I could not blame anyone for this repeated cycle it was a ferocious cycle that I could not seem to break free from. I was going to church bleeding and confused and shattered into a million pieces. I tried to keep the church face on and tried to mask the appearance of what I was really dealing with. I was the one wearing the "mask" trying to maintain a certain image and trying to conceal the reality of what was really going on inside of me. Which many of us do. We cover up and have a mask on. We hide what really going on inside of us. We compensate with our outer appearances but our internal be jacked up. I know for me growing up we were taught that you pray and leave it there. We were not taught to get counseling or professional help. We were taught what happens in your home stay in your home. Many have lived in pain for so many years like me. Not having a place of escape. Many people feel hopeless like I did and do not know which way to turn. It was not about me going to church anymore when I did not have a real relationship with God. I went out of routine and yes, I felt stronger when I went. But my lifestyle and my character were all tore up.

Well, that not the end of my story. I was faced head-on with an identity crisis and it was beginning to show even more. I carried my emotions in my face and in body language. And people began to see the brokenness but yet I still did not get the help I needed. No matter how much I tried to talk to different ones and tried to get counseling. I was often misunderstood and judged. Instead of getting me help I was often criticized, judged, and marked for it. That why it so important to find a safe haven. A place where you can feel safe and be fully confident that what you share with someone it stays safe with them. And it not carried out in the street like your garbage or using as a sermon spoken

Dream Again After the Identity Crisis

on a Wednesday night or being spoken on a Sunday morning message across the pulpit. The church supposed to be a healing center. You just do not know people stories. Do not use it as leverage over them. I can attest that I experienced that as well. Nobody cannot feel what you feel. What you experience or encounter is yours, not anyone else's. They may have a similarity or may have some knowledge of what you may have experience, but the reality is they not you and cannot feel what you feel about your life. They did not experience your traumas. So, it vexes me to hear people say move on, get over it, you should know better etc. yes, we should move pass our mistakes. But when there is years and layers of pain. It may take longer for those of us to get our healing. Every walk is different just like our genetic makeups are different. Every fingerprint is different. We as people come in all shapes and sizes and we often compared by looking at someone else through a one-sided lens. We cannot compare and critique someone else. Who are we to judge, and pick apart someone else life and their process? I have experienced it from the world and from the church arena.

Matthew 7:1-4 - *Do not judge, or you too will be judged. 2For in the same way, you judge others, you will be judged, and with the measure you use, it will be measured to you. 3Why do you look at the speck of sawdust into your brother's eye and pay no attention to the plank in your own eye? 4How can you say to your brother, 'Let me take the speck out of your eye,' when all the time there is a plank in your own eye?*

Do you truly know who you are? And why you do the things you do?
_____
_____
_____
_____
_____

Dream Again After the Identity Crisis

Have you ever been misunderstood, judged or critique by someone?

How did it make you feel?

Do you have a safe place or have a safe person to share your most intimate concerns with? And do you trust them to keep it confidential?

7 | THE TRIP UP & THE AFTERMATH: WHERE DO I GO FROM HERE?

In, 2008, I got free from that marriage and began to start focusing on rededicating myself to the Lord once again. One thing about God He is a loving Father and is just to forgiving us for our sins. God no matter how many times we fall He will forgive us over and over again. No matter how many times we fall He will open his arms up to us. Especially when we are sincerely ready. Trying to gain a relationship and a sense of peace for myself. I began to walk alone and tried to recovery from all that transpired in the previous years of my life. God put me in a new place and a new church where I can be taught the principle of Godly living. During this transition God began to clean me up from the inside out little by little and It did not happen all at one. I stop running and seeking. I really needed to try to focus on my dedication to the things of God. Right Afterr the divorce God called me into the ministry which I always knew that I had a call on my life. I just did not want it or know what to do with it. But God said He wanted to use me I always knew but just could not see myself being used. How can God use me when my life was so messy, and I couldn't even see myself during any type of ministering to anyone period? I was a wrench undone. But finally took heed to the call I was doing okay for almost two years Afterr the marriage ended even though I had ups and downs along the way. I am not going even lie it was a struggle trying to be the person God had called for me to but at least I wanted to try. Which I did not have much of a clue as to what that entailed. All the

Dream Again After the Identity Crisis

while still struggling to survive and overcome my desires and pitfalls.

A couple years later in 2010, I got caught up in a sex trap it was laid up for me and I ran right into it why because I was not delivered from that perverse spirit. That was a thorn in my flesh wanting a having a relationship. I ran into an old male friend that I had not seen in a many of years from back in the day when my daughter was born. And the connection happened inside of a restaurant on a New Year's Day. We talked for a good while and exchange information and saw each other regularly until one day I found out the He was still married. Here I go being caught up in a marital affair. When I confronted him, He told me he was separated and getting a divorce from the spouse. So, with my naïve self, I am believing the lies. I was not using good judgment nor was I using discernment. I should have been paying attention to the pattern, but I did not. I tried to close that door but on valentine day that same year. He comes by to visit me and bring me a gift and guess what I fell back into his arms and melted from the attention that he given me. Those traps the enemy send they can be so deceitful, and the spirit of deception is so real. And it came back with a vengeance when you open those doors back up. At this point, I opened the door to be fooled all over again. I just was not learning my lesson. And this time I had a hard time in closing the door completely. Even my ex-husband was still lingering around and was trying to make me feeling pity and guilt for exiting our relationship so much so that when I transition to my new church, he followed me there and he joined the church to monitor me. It was like I could not get that one big break. I attended a conference that I was invited to by someone. And while at this service God began to deal with me there about the closure of my relationship with my ex. It was hard to put closure on him because he was always around it was like a yoke. He vexed me every time he was in my presence. It was so bad to where he even had the nerve to start bringing a young lady to church with him. Which opened more doors of hurt, anger, and frustration in me. In the back of my mind, I was asking why the marriage did not work. I was mad at him and God. I felt mad and anger because I could not fully heal from the residue and the sting of the marriage. Let me point this out to get back to the point of the other man that I was trying to stay connected to. He came into my life while I was still trying to recover from the dissolved marriage. See the enemy has plots and plans as well. And he knew my

Dream Again After the Identity Crisis

weakness and he found a crack door open in my life and I illegally let him in. I can confess this today another self-inflicted moment because of the brokenness and disobedience in my life. It was so bad that I did not even realize consciously or subconsciously how bad this spirit was operating in me. Moments of weakness and being flesh lead can lead you into dangerous paths. When I tried to finally break free from my ex. The enemy already had the next bait around the corner waiting for me and I got immediately attached to it. Crazy, right! You would have thought I learned some lessons by now. I caused more damage to my mind, my heart, and my soul, and had no more fight in me. When I was trying to close the door on them both. I felt like I died inside. I felt emptiness all over again and I felt like I had let God down as whereas the ministry that I was in. I grieved some badly over those relationships as if someone had died in my life. I yearn and crave the relationship behind closed doors and still tried to fake it and make it in the church. My deceptions were a trap for me. I wanted this man to be my husband I wanted him to leave his wife. I tried to imagine in my mind what it would be like if we were together. Even though I was not seeing him anymore physically but was still mentally attached. That soul tie was a deep one. I was like how did I get here again. And why did I allow this to happen to me again. How did I let this thing go so far, I was so far from God! This man became my idol and lover I replaced him for God. It got so deep and real to me. My flesh was operating in full- force because of this door opening. I became promiscuous on a whole other level. I became a lover of my own self. I was a hot mess in the inside, and it displayed on the outside.

Now, I must suffer the consequences of my actions. I did not even know how to get back in right standard with the Father. I could not see or feel the love of my father God anymore. I was just hurting in so many areas. When I asked God for forgiveness, in the beginning, I felt so low and did not even feel the same. I could not even pray the way I use to. I could not feel him in my atmosphere anymore. It was hard to get back to that intimate place with God. When I tried to get into my secret place with God it was a struggle. It almost felt like God had put me on trial in court. He wanted to see how I was going to treat him again and if I was ready to completely surrender myself to him. And not put another man before him. The pain, the pain was so hurtful I cannot even imagine how God felt about my actions. And how God viewed me. He seen me going in such a destructive path. He had begun to start the healing process in me to set me free. But I went right back into the worldly things. Now I have to seek until I find him and allow him to teach me all over again. I had to ask for understanding, I had to find the root cause of my actions. I had to step back and re-evaluate my life. I felt as if the disappointment that I was feeling God was feeling the same. I knew God still loved me. I just did not know him as my Abba Father. I began to realize because I did not have the love of my natural father, that I did not know how to love God as my father either. Not only did I affect myself, but it affected my leaders, the people who looked up to me in ministry and I felt like I let my family down even though they did not have a clue as to what was going on with my life. It was just not about me anymore or about what Sherronda wanted. I was weaker than a newborn puppy and no identity in sight.

How many times have we gone against God's will? But yet He still forgive us. Do you believe God can forgive you of your sins?

_____
_____
_____
_____

Have you forgiving yourself or are you holding yourself hostage by continuing to condemn yourself?

_____
_____
_____
_____

Dream Again After the Identity Crisis

What if God tells you "No" not yet will you still you believe and trust him? Even when it hurt will you remain humble and steadfast?

_____
_____
_____
_____
_____

What have/or has been your response to God when you didn't' or don't get the expected answers you are looking for?

_____
_____
_____
_____
_____

8 | MIDNIGHT CRY!! LORD CAN YOU HEAR ME?

Will I ever see the dawning of a new day? All I could see was darkness all around me and I could not see my future. Nor could I see the plans God had in stored for me.

As **Jeremiah 29:11** declares. *"For I know the plans I have for you," declares the Lord. "plans to prosper you and not to harm you, plans to give you hope and a future.*

I just knew in my mind that God did not want to use me anymore. How can God use me a wrench like me a filthy rag I was, a girl with so many past mistakes and so much bad history? I was feeling so frazzled! But was yet determined to try to overcome. Some people have told me to get over my past let my past be my past. But when you have not gotten true deliverance you go through repeats such as what I had encountered. Years of brokenness, traumas, and abuse in the areas of, mental, physical, psychologically, and spiritually. When you deal with psychological instabilities it causes you to not know who you are as person. Yet alone who you are in Christ. I was unstable in so many ways, deliverance is what I needed. And I truly thought I had demons living in me I probably did. All I knew was those inner demons keep me bound. I had talked to a few people, but no one understood my cry or the depths of my pain it ran deep. I stayed connected to the church because I felt like that was my lifeline. And if I left the church I would die or go right back to the ways of the world. I wanted to have a real dedicated and consecrated life wholeheartedly for God but the devasting issues keep tripping me up and it was happening to me over and over. God do you see me, do you see me, or hear me? I am crying in desperation and I need your help to rescue me from my self. I was my own worst enemy. My inner man was depleted. But keeping busy in the church house to keep me out of trouble and dangers. What do I do now? The very one that I needed love and help from now needs me? Help me Lord.

In 2008, I also find out my mom was sick. We did not have much of a bond at all. And now I have to help her as much as I can. The very one whom I felt rejected and abandon by. Being the fact that she was still my mother. I felt obligated as a daughter to be there for her. She battled colon cancer and that was a hard for me to comprehend. Even though my mom was not there for me like I would have wanted from her. I knew I had to be there for her doing her battle of sickness. I went through some challenges even in that. I never felt the validation or love from my parents and that where my initial pain all started. Now finding myself having to care for someone whom I felt did not love me was a hard pill I had to swallow. Now I have to give my love to her on her bed of affliction. Around 2010-2011, I tried to build a bond with my mom in her last years of living. I began to forgive her during this time before she would transition. I did not want her to close her eyes and her heart stop beating without her knowing that I loved her. God gave me the strength to be in the room alone with her the day she died. It was an amazing day, and I was at peace and I believe she was too. The night she passed I was afraid to go to sleep because I wanted to hold her hand when she took her last breath. I remember the nurse came in the room and said Ms. Ross you must be exhausted you been here all day and you been by your mom's side none stop. She said she is in good hand why do not you go home or take a nap. We will keep her comfortable. Of course, I was not going to leave the hospital. So, I moved my chair from her bed to the wall and leaned my head back. I dozed off for about ten to fifteen mins. And while I was in a rest state the most amazing thing happened. I saw myself on an empty train. I can feel the motion of the train moving. It was so relaxing and after a few minutes of riding. I get a tap on my shoulder it the nurse telling me she is gone that she had transitioned. I was like wow I truly believe God allowed me to feel the peaceful transition in the form of a train ride. Every time I think about that night it makes me emotional to this day.

Exodus 20:12 Honor thy father and mother: that thy days may be long upon the land which the Lord thy God giveth thee.

If you were in a position to care for a loved one that you felt did not love you how would you handle that?

_____
_____
_____
_____
_____

Do you ever feel like God not hearing your prayers?

_____
_____
_____
_____
_____

What does the bible say about honoring our parents?

_____
_____
_____
_____
_____

Dream Again After the Identity Crisis

Have you ever felt obligated to do something for someone who did not care for you or about you? How did you treat the matter?

_____
_____
_____
_____
_____

1 Timothy 5:8 - *Anyone who does not provide for their relatives, and especially for their own household, has denied the faith and is worse than an unbeliever.*

9 | THE PATH TO UNLOCKING MY DREAMS

Afterr the passing of my mother in 2012, I begin searching for answers to regain my strength and wanted to start a spiritual journey to pursue the things of God. I married for a third time but this time I did not pursue him, and I am still with my current husband. We have been married now for nine years that the longest I've be in a committed relationship. Through we've have some bumps, bruises, and hardship along the way we still remain together by the help of the Lord. Many times, did I want to throw in the towel in this relationship too, but I was determining to allow God to work things out for us. One of the things I had to do was work on me and not be so focus on the things I was seeing and hearing in my atmosphere that were not so good in my marriage. At one time in my life, I magnified the issues of my relationship and always wanted to point out the not so good of my mate. I could not see the specks in my own eye. I was quick to point out his mishaps and his so-called dirt's. And did not acknowledge the damage that I was doing too. I was in a prideful place and did not want to admit my ways either. God has been dealing with me and He wanted me to see me not him. He wanted me to start seeing him as Christ sees him in spite of his flaws. I had to let go of my bitterness, anger, and stubbornness of remaining a victim of the abuse that I always felt. I had to learn that I could not always judge him or be so critical of his issues. I had to realize I was not my pain or needing to live in that place anymore. I had to begin to see that I can

Dream Again After the Identity Crisis

live again and dream again and be who God created me to be. Another thing I had to realized is that I had unrealistic expectations and that was told to me several times, but I just could see that I was doing that. The things I desired or wanted may not have been necessary things my spouse could give me or fulfill for me.

We sometimes put our focus on the wrong things or expect others to fill voids that we lack in. It defitnely was an eye opener for me and it took some soul searching to get me to a place where I can have a little since of peace. It took a long time for me to see that part of me that was still damaged. I needed to break free from the expectation of man to fulfill my happiness. Only the true and living God can give you that type of peace, joy, and fullness of happiness through Him. I had to reprogram my thinking and open my heart to receive the changes. I have now begun to work on me to find myself worth and have begun to work on some inner self-healing. I needed to allow God to be my everything, my Jireh-my provider and not expecting my spouse or other people to be my rescuer. I am depending on everyone else to fix me and my issues. I tried that and it failed miserably so I had to make a change. I started focusing on my inner peace something that was much needed in my life and I needed to become somewhat stress free. I shifted my mindset and now on a new journey called finding me. To find myself and my new identity in Christ Jesus is long overdue. No longer waiting or wanting man's approval or validation to tell me who I am. But allowing God to show me who I am and how He feels about me. Allowing the Father to mend the broken pieces of my life. Allowing Him to be my Father and mother when I need Him to be. Allowing Him to comfort and love me the way I need to be loved. Allowing Him to touch the places where I felt empty. He is the ultimate one. He is that everything we need Him to be in our lives. I just needed to know it for myself. I wanted to change and striving daily to work on my relationship with God so I can get free and stay free from my past. I had to get my mind focused, and my heart fixed. It was a heart issue for me. My heart was sick, and my mind was disturbed.

But one thing I always desired was to be healed. No matter what it took, no matter how long it took, the main thing is getting there. I had to do this for myself and not for anyone. Even in this process I had to remove somethings out in my life. And if it is for me to have it God

Dream Again After the Identity Crisis

will open it up again.

But until God say so I will not move even when if it hurt. I cannot move until God instructs for so long, I moved in what I wanted not necessarily what God wanted me to have. It took a lot of praying, crying out to God, fasting, and getting help with my pains. I sort out getting professional help and received spiritual counseling through my leader that God placed me under. I set some goals for myself, believed in myself, and start trusting the process to get my healing. I did not want to rush it this time around I wanted to see positive results and I want them to stick. I had to pursue and give up my own will. I have been working hard to get me to where I am today. There were many things I dreamed about and wanted to do for such a long time but did not know how to obtain them. I always wanted to do something for myself and God. Soul searching for me was necessary to help me grow. I had to dig deep and get to the root of my cycles, patterns, and pain. I began to seek God and ask Him to show me how He views me. I had to start speaking affirmations over myself. I asked God to show me what I can do in my life that could be a blessing to other women especially who have experience traumas in their life. I always loved people and was always willing to serve in any capacity within the church and in my local community. I always loved to bless individuals and wanted to put a smile on their faces through my gifts, and talents. In spite of what my feeling were. I always made a conscience effort to help others to see their happiness over mines. But I cannot neglect my happiness anymore that was not a good Idea. I thought if I helped others It would bring me great pleasure in their times of need. Do not get me wrong I love helping but was I doing it in a healthy way. Well not all the time. I 've always wanted to be committed and wanted to be submitted to my local church and support my family to the best of my ability. I continued to pray and ask God to allow me to dream again and to find my true identity. The things that I endured never caused me to lose my hope in God. I wanted to challenge myself to do better and to be better. The journey to my healing is happening little by little step by step. Trying to be more focused on allowing my gifts and talents to make room for me in the way God see fit not me going before Him. There is a saying that the old folks use to say, "If I can just help one somebody that is good enough for me." For many years, my life was at a halt because I had my focus on raising my daughter and trying to be

Dream Again After the Identity Crisis

that humble servant to the church and supporting family insuring that everything would be alright.

Today, I believe I am in a better place and trying my best to be a better mother to my daughter. She is my top priority. I put a lot of my dreams on hold. But now that she is older and have fewer medical needs, I started venturing out to do somethings for myself to boost my confidence and to feel a sense of self-worth. God is beginning to unlock doors and unlocking giftings, He is giving me creative ideas that I dare not take credit for. Because I have been listening and receiving wise counsel, I am able to utilize the tools given to me. By making necessary changes I am now making dreams become realities for my life. One thing I did for myself was I started taking some classes in an area that I was familiar with which was caregiving. I got a job Afterr not working outside the home for many years. I became a licensed personal care aide then further got my medical assistance aide certificates. And now, I am a licensed-sponsored residential provider for disabled adults in the State of Virginia. I am so glad that I did not give up on myself because surely there was a sense of hope and not despair. I now recognized that my life was not over and that it was just beginning for me. What seems delayed is not always a denial. Our timing is not like God. His timing is perfect. Though things got delayed it was not denied.

Realizing now, that I could do anything that I desired with the help of the Lord. Even if I have to do it differently from others. Seeing things from a different perspective to better my life. Knowing that I can be better, live better, and do better. Not only that, but I also had to come to the realization that I deserved better.

Finally, starting to see some light and feeling like I have accomplished a little something makes me proud of myself. As I am getting stronger and building up, I have to keep my focus on God and do what He asked of me. I have to stay in my own lane and stay faithful to that because there were times though I was doing so much for home and church, I still felt a level of emptiness and depletion. The missing link was that I was still struggling with my identity it was a place that I could not seem to find. Working in the church having my hands in everything. Helping in every way I can to fill voids. I was serving from a place of gratitude and love for God, but yet was still bleeding. By being in a new place this time around I wanted to live for Christ all the way and know who I am in a real way, learning who I am and learning how God uses me has been a game changer for my life. And I do not have to compare myself to others anymore and I do not have to worry about how they are doing it. I can just be me in my action, thoughts, and deeds being my true authentic self. He made all of us different and we all have different ways of during things.

The reality is my identity was missing for a very long time and the not knowing what my role was in the church was lacking. That was a constant battle I fought within because I always knew there was a level of ministry that I would have to do one day. There was an internal war going on. This walk has truly not been easy. In the beginning, I ran from it. and to be honest sometimes still do not want it because of all the things I had to experienced. I was judged by so many people, even church leaders, I have experienced being talked about, criticized, and mocked, scorn, and often publicly humiliated because of what they knew, seen, or heard concerning my life, or about my marriage. I was openly shamed and humiliated right in the church. The very place where I suppose to have been receiving healing and guidance. It ended up being a battleground. Keeping the good fight of faith, I kept pressing, pushing and pursuing. It took me to get connected to some other individuals to pray for me, counsel me, and to cover me when I could not cover myself. I had to seek out some mentors that could push me into my purpose. I had to do it so I would not lose my faith in God or result back to my past. That is what carried me through. In the year of 2017, God saw fit to elevate me to the office of an Elder. I was just as confused as to why He promoted me. I was like God with all I been through and how I was feeling. I cannot believe that you would see fit move me to another level. I did not have a clue as to what the role of an Elder was. Now, do not get me wrong I was serving diligently and was faithful with the local assembly that I was in at that time. But my relationship with God was still hit and misses. There were still parts of me I still needing healing in and it was stagnating me from moving forward. My personal struggles keep me stagnated. I was dealing with hurts from home and within the church. No, the church did not hurt me, and I would never say that. But sometimes individuals and uncompassionate leaders within a church can contribute to the

Dream Again After the Identity Crisis

hurts because you are hurting. And with that being said, let us move into another topic. I started traveling to get away to have moments of tranquility in order to reflect, refocus, and redo some things. I was constantly searching for that peace that I could not seem to find.

One Sunday morning, God met me in my bedroom and gave me a dream this dream shifted my entire life for the embitterment of my growth and stability. It was if God himself said enough daughter you have been through enough in this place and now it time for me to take you to a new place; so, that you can heal and grow effectively. I took heed to what was shown to me and I decided to walk blind. I walked by faith to move into a new and fresh start. I was so ready. I had cried so many tears asking the Lord to hear my cries and come to my rescue. I often prayed to God asking Him to give me a fresh start. I needed to be in a place where no one knew me or my past. I need to be where I could hear God clearly. I knew deep inside if I was to walk out the path, He was calling me to I had to shift. My life depending on it. During my time of transitioning God called me by name and confirmed that which He showed me. And He said to me it was time. He showed me what to do and as to where my new place was for me to go. He told me that in this place, I would be safe and find refuge. All that He revealed it happening just like that. Fearful and all but I know without a shadow of a doubt that it was imperative to be obedient to the shift, so I did. When I shifted my ears opened and my heart received, my ears were no longer deaf, and my heart was no longer numb. Further being able to use my gifts and talents for Him.

In 2018, God birthed my first level of ministry. I was able to support, and help disabled adults and their families. I never realized until then, that your greatest passions and gifts are a part of your ministry. Just like what you go through is not just for you it for somebody else. Your testimony is your testimony, and your transparency can help someone else get set free and delivered. I always had a passion for people with disabilities because I knew first-hand what it was like as a caregiver. I had the opportunity to establish a nonprofit that supports families and minister to those families about God. Another door unlocked for me during my transition Afterr being in the new place for two years. I was able to serve and help those in need. That was my niche and I loved to do it. I never correlated that this gift of hospitality was

Dream Again After the Identity Crisis

ministry too and it was already in full operation I just did not have a full understanding of what to do with it. I never piece together that it was part of the ministry God had for me to do. So, it nothing wrong with being a servant it actually was a humbling experience for me. I originally thought it was just a talent God gave me (an eye opener for me) and I enjoyed doing it. Even though, I went through a rough patch. The occurrences this time around hit different. I had to be determined that what happened to me would not carry on with me to the new place that God had sent me too. It tried to form but God did not allow it to penetrate me. Every battle scar was necessary, and it was for my making and it had to push me into another level maturity. To becoming an adult not the little scared girl I once was. I was needing to grow up in many areas of my life and still a work in progress. I needed restoration and God is bringing it to me now. I could not see me getting what I needed before, but I am glad that I am receiving what I needed now. Biblical, sound, and practical teachings is essential in a personal life as well as not being judgmental. My flaws are not being magnified and I finally filling the Love of God. The level of intimacy I desired to give the Lord and Him back to me is finally opening up in a greater way. He is validating me because He chose me, called me, and have need of me. Whatever I can do to please God is what I want to do. He has needs of my hands, mouth, and my feet. I just want to please His heart. And hear him say in the end Well done thy good and faithful servant.

I am dreaming again, and my desires are truly being fulfilled. Things I said many years ago that I wanted to do is coming to life. I am gaining my strength back in Christ Jesus. I am gaining confidence that was once lost, I am gaining my peace that was once taken. I am learning my true authentic identity in Christ Jesus. I was afraid to live in a life of freedom, but freedom belongs to me. It is God's will that we prosper and be in good health. My self-esteem was very low, and I could not see my worth and the lack caused some unhealthy way to arise. I was doing for everybody else except myself. I could not do for me because I did not know me. I had no good path to follow. "But God", He always supplied all of my needs. He saw that it was a need for me to learn more of Him. So, I could learn more of who He made me to be. I always loved the Lord with my whole heart I just had some lack of loving myself.

Dream Again After the Identity Crisis

I was called "A Courageous Warrior" back in 2020. I did not fully understand the meaning of why God called me that until one day the person said because you always bounce back. As I began to ponder on that -- I am like you are right. God has always kept me through the goods and the not so goods of my life. He has always kept me even in my lowest valley. The enemy is a destiny killer and he wanted to destroy my life. And that was from birth all the way to my adulthood. He tried to make me forfeit my destiny and my assignments. He tried to block me from living in my full potential, but God said not so. Today I can testify of no goodness of my own but right now in this moment, right here!! Let me just stop right here and Give God a great big praise. He has brought me over every time. Hallelujah!! I thank Him for the lessons I have had to learn and the lessons I am still learning. When I think back over my life and think things over, I can truly say that I have been blessed of the goodness of the Lord. I truly thank Him for every test and trial. I thank Him for allowing me an opportunity to share a piece of my life with you. This was my process and my story Dream Again Afterr the Identity Crisis.

Jeremiah 29:11 declares these words, *"For I know the plans I have for you," declares the Lord, "plans to prosper you and not to harm you, plans to give you hope and a future.*

I do not know all the details of God's intended plan for my life, nor do I know what the future holds for me, but I know I am well on my way to having a victorious life in Christ Jesus. For truly He is the author and finisher of my faith. He is Alpha and Omega, the beginning and the end. He said that I was going to live again, and dream again, and not die and that one day I would declare his word and speak of His goodness. And that brings me into how God changed my name from Sherronda to my "beloved daughter". He said He has great need of me.

It does not matter how great or small it would be. God can use all of us and He has a purpose and plan for all of our lives. We may not see the fulness of where n He wants to take us. But just Go with what He wants, and you cannot go wrong in that.

Dream Again After the Identity Crisis

I could not give up on God because He did not give up on me. He is always moving on our behalf and He will not give up on you either. It only takes that one step first of repenting of our sins, forgiving ourselves, forgiving others, and letting go of our past mistakes that keeps us hostage.

Romans 8:1 - *Therefore, there is no condemnation for those who are in Christ Jesus. So, we do not have to feel guilty, shameful, or beat ourselves up or let anyone else hold us hostage from our past mistakes. If you want to be healed ask God.*

Psalms 147:3 - *He Heals the brokenhearted and binds up their wounds.*

Mark 9:23- *"Jesus said unto him, If thou canst believe, all things are possible to him that believeth."*

Do you believe God can heal you? _____
_____
_____
_____
_____

What area in your life are you struggling with and needing ABBA Father to heal?
_____
_____
_____
_____

What area in your life that you can admit that you need to total surrender to Him?
_____
_____
_____
_____

Dream Again After the Identity Crisis

What is one thing you would like to do in your life that you have not accomplished yet?

_____
_____
_____
_____
_____

Dream Again After the Identity Crisis
What Helped Me to Heal?

Eight lessons were learned during my process that has help my growth and development:

1. I had stand on the promises of God and when He spoke a thing, it would come to past. Not when I wanted it to happen but in His timing.

2. I had to learn even through oppositions. God would see me through. So even when my back was up against a wall. God would not let me fall.

3. I had to learn that my life was not over, and that God had much need of me and a purpose for my life. Even when I did not see it or know how it was going to turn out God has the final say.

4. I had to know that God would calm every storm. When my life seems like it was raging and in turbulence. He would make my every crooked place straight. When I surrendered whole heartily and yield completely the healing began to take place.

5. When I find my place in Him, He begin to show me who I am. And is showing me what I should and should not do. He will never steer me wrong.

6. I had to learn that it was okay to seek professional help to deal with my pain outside of the church. As well as seek help from my senior leader and to be held accountable.

7. I had to begin to start speaking positive affirmation over myself. I had to start declaring God word over me and motivating myself to live again.

8. Lastly, I had to believe that I can do all things through Christ that strengthens me. I had to fight for my life and for my sanity.

10 | I'M COMING OUT / THE COMEBACK

On a summer day in June 2020, I was sitting on my patio just talking to God about somethings and He spoke back to my spirit so clearly. As I was talking to him, I told him I did not want women to experience what I have gone through. As we already known, women can be emotional human being and we can carry a lot of responsibilities on our plates on a daily. As I God speaking to him, I am asking Him how I can be a blessing to women like me who have dealt with brokenness or how can I serve woman who have experience different levels of pain that don't have a safe place to express themselves. And as I was sitting, I began to draw from that place in which I knew best on how to do and that was serve and share in my gifting of hospitality. I wanted to have a place where we as women could come together let our hair down and have a breathier to destress from the cares of life. I wanted to create a space where they can chat and have some creative activities to make them feel special, and or appreciated. From what I thought was another business adventure God shifted it right into a ministry. Again, I could never see how what I already had inside me would be a ministering opportunity. And that where we sometimes miss it. I always felt that helping and encouraging women who experienced brokenness in their life would be a good fit for me. Be it trauma in their marriages, or in their families, or personal relationship. I always had a passion to see women set free from their pains just like me. For years, I suffered unnecessarily but did not also have the proper tools to help me get free either. I wanted to see myself delivered and now wanting other ladies to get their healing and deliverance too.

On July 25th, God did just what I asked him, I birthed Something Delightful Empowerment for Women, a safe place where women can come together and share their issues and release their pains. A place where we can release and get the proper healing that we need and help support each other together. Even though, I went through what I went through it was to help others too. As my life began to change, I am learning now that my level of influence can change the lives of women through my transparency and by the telling of my story.

Now, that you have read my story could you identify and patterns or cycles in your own life and if so, write it out?

_____
_____
_____
_____

Have you ever asked yourself what makes me be the way I am or what makes me do what I do?

_____
_____
_____
_____

Did you identify some root causes of your cycles? What have been some of your stumbling blocks? Who or what do you have an illegal allegiance too?

_____
_____
_____
_____

Dream Again After the Identity Crisis

Are you doing all that you can for yourself to break free and become whole?

_____
_____
_____
_____
_____

I cannot give no one else glory or credit regarding God unfolding my dreams and making them into reality. I am striving to walk in this new place daily, and in this place; it is something beautiful. I am living again and dreaming again Afterr such a devastating crisis throughout my 46 years of living.

I finally "Becoming" and Coming Out - - Becoming into who and what God says I am and coming out of bondage to be what He called of me to be.

Luke 4:18 says *The Spirit of the Lord is on me, because he has appointed me to proclaim good news to the poor. He has sent me to proclaim freedom for those prisoners and recovery of sight for the blind, to set the oppressed free.*

We do not have to be slaves or prisoners of our past. I am a living witness that God can transform us. He can turn our mess into a message. God loves us so much, He want us to have a life full of Love, Joy, Peace, and Happiness! And if we do not have that we need to find that place in him. It is in Christ that we walk in total (complete) Healing in every area of our lives. Complete Healing, Complete Deliverance, Complete Freedom, And complete Victory. It all belongs to us and we can have it if we want it.

"You can Be Free"
"You can Dream Again"
"You can Live Again"
Be Who God called you to be unapologetically.

Dream Again After the Identity Crisis

Declarations:
I declare and decree that you shall live and not die, I declare and decree that you will be successful in all that purpose yourself to do, I declare and decree that God will sustain you and keep you, I declare and decree that you shall be the head and not the tail. You shall be above and not beneath. And that you shall walk in the ways of God and do all that you find your hands to do.

You are beautiful no matter what they say word or life issues cannot bring you down!! You are fearfully and wonderful made!!

Closing Encouragement & Closing Prayer:
It just takes a willingness and a determination to allow God to heal and cleanse us from the inside out. I pray you got something out of my story, and I pray that if you are dealing with unresolved issues of pain that you would release them and get the proper help that you need. You do not have to stay stuck. If I had not shifted in my life to get me to my new place. I would not have been able to see some of the things that God had for me or called for me to do in this season of my life.

God specializes He is the ultimate one that goes before us. He will be our Strength. our Provider, our Comforter, our Helper, and our Guide.

My prayer for each of us is to be healed!
Heavenly Father, I pray that everyone that reads this book is touched by you and that if it is anything is us that needs to be healed or if there is any residue of a sting from our past that it be eradicated and no longer hold us captive. Be healed in Jesus Name. I pray that every driving force that causes us repeats and cycles in our life be gone from us. I pray that every diabolical attack of the enemy be lose off of us in Jesus Name. And I call forth Freedom, Liberty, and Wholeness to come forth in our lives in Christ Jesus name. I pray the bind of wickedness no longer a part of our DNA. But the Love of Jesus Christ be upon our lives. I pray that we will walk with our heads up high and smiles on our faces. I pray that we will live out our lives with love, joy, and peace. I pray that we will live in the ways of God knowing our true identities. No longer having those hinderance and over blockages over our shoulders and in our hearts. I pray that we release them and let them go. I pray we give everything over to you Lord every weight, concern, and matter. I pray that we will give it

Dream Again After the Identity Crisis

over to you a place of surrender so you can heal us.

And to the person that reading this book that may not have a relationship with God or have backslidden away from him. I pray that you have a desire to get to know God and or come back into right standards with him. God is a forgiver of our sins and He does not hold our past against us, nor does he condemn us for them. If you need salvation in your life it is available to you today. According to the word of God you can make this confessing and it will change your life for the better.

Romans 10:9-11 (NIV) 9*If you declare with your mouth," Jesus is Lord," and believe in your heart that God raised him from the dead, you will be saved. 10For it is with your heart that you believe and are justified, and it is with your mouth that you profess your faith and are saved. As Scripture says, 11"Anyone who believes in him will never be put to shame.*

It is as simply put confess this with me. Lord Jesus, I ask you to come into my heart and forgive me of my sins. I believe and confess with my own mouth that you are Lord. I believe that you died and was raised from the died. I believe right now in my heart that Jesus is Lord over my life. I believe that my sins are forgiven. And that you have given me a clean slate. Believe it in this very moment of your confession that you are Saved by the Power of Jesus Christ our Lord. Amen and it is so!!

John 14:14 - says that *we can ask anything in your name, and you will do it.*
We declare and decree our freedom that place and hindrance that has keep us stagnated and caused us not to grow be removed in Jesus Mighty name.

John 8:36 – tells us, *if the Son sets you free, you will be free indeed.*

So, we give our issues and our pains to the Son of the Living God believe and stand on his word.

Galatians 5:1 - *It is for freedom that Christ has set us free.*
Stand firm, then, and do not let yourselves be burdened again by a yoke of slavery.

Dream Again After the Identity Crisis

I pray that we will be confident and have faith that everything is going work out for our good. God loves us with and everlasting love. It is His will that we prosper and be in good health. Healthy and whole in every part of our lives.

Be courageous your life is not over. If you should ever feel like your life is over it not. God has the final say. You can bounce back. You may even feel like your life is being dribbled, like a basketball. Being bounced to and fro. You may feel like your life is shattered in a million pieces; it is not. Know, that God can jumpstart your life all over again. Let God cultivate you into something new.

Blessing in Christ Jesus,
Sherronda Ross-Brown, Author

The sole intentions of this book are to help bring awareness to women who may have experienced trauma in your life, and you do not know what to do or where to find refuge or healing. For those women that have lost your way. You may feel like all hope is lost. You may feel like you cannot start over. You may feel like yours dreams, desires and or passions are gone. Well, this is for you! I want to tell you that your life is not over. Once you identify what is affecting you and recognize the cycles in your life that may have caused you some repeats or misfortunes to turn it into life lessons and pick yourself back up.

Dream Again you are not dead, but yet alive.
Get Free, Be Free, and Stay Free!! In Jesus Mighty Name!

BIOGRAPHY OF AUTHOR, SHERRONDA ROSS-BROWN

Sherronda Ross-Brown was born and raised in the church and got baptized at age 12. As a child, she served and sang in many local churches, under the direction of her late Grandmother Bishop Viola Reynolds of Gethsemane Holiness Church in Richmond, VA. She is a wife, and mother of a loving daughter G'Nelle who is dear to her heart. Sherronda never have let anything stop her from dreaming or pursuing her goals. She is multi-talented and is the proud owner of several businesses which are SweetBells Creations where she showcases her creative gifting through event & party planning. Another one of her businesses is We Care Resources Group for Disabled Adults and their Families, where she is the CEO. This ministry is a nonprofit, where she supports disabled adults and their families within her local community with activities and resources. Sherronda accepted the commission of ministry in 2008, where she was licensed as a minister under the late Robert M. Brunson Jr. of Unlimited Power Transformation Church. Later years on June 4th, 2017, she was elevated into the office of an Elder, under the leadership of Bishop Duane Bell of New Destiny Apostolic Church. In 2018, God shifted her, and she transitioned into a new ministry to help her grow and to be cultivated into her new phase of ministry. She is currently a member of Made in His Image International Ministries under tutelage of Dr. Apostle Valarie and Pastor Lynn Jackson in Oxon Hill, MD. Sherronda is a courageous warrior that title was given to her back in 2020. Sherronda faced many obstacles, but always found a way to bounce back. Sherronda loves to travel and has been in international waters. Some places she has experienced in her travels were Belize, Aruba, Jamaica, Puerto Rico, Bahamas just to name a few. She would love to do more traveling overseas and would like to venture into during some mission's trip in the near future. Sherronda loves to be a blessing and gives from her heart and loves to put a smile on the faces of others she comes in contact with. Sherronda loves her family and have one sister Marca Ross-Nicholl of Lawrenceville, GA who faithfully supports her. Sherronda has four nieces and two nephews and one great-nephew.

She has had many mentors over the past years and would like to honor each of them for covering her during some challenging times in her life. They prayed, supported, and counseled her in their own perspective places. Apostle Valerie Jackson, Apostle Trena Stephenson, Apostle-elect Lisa Veney, Pastor Robert & lady Fran Mitchell, Bishop Duane & Pastor Patricia Bell, and Pastor Elicia Brunson. If it were not for these individuals, she does not know where she would be today. While embarking on her spiritual journey, God birthed a ministry through her pain, and trauma, which brings us to this current time. Something Delightful Empowerment for Women (SDEFW) was birthed in such a unique way. SDEFW, so she thought was just an activity for women to just get together to let their hair down, relax, and fellowship with one another from time to time. The first gathering was held July 2020 at Sherronda's home where she had a garden party for a group of women. Another activity God gave her was a paint and sip event for the women. During this fellowship, God allowed her an opportunity to pour into the ladies. Because of the hospitality shown to them, she received comments and feedback from the women to keep it going. Through these events, God showed her that there was a greater purpose. The purpose is to support women of brokenness. Being open to the Holy Spirit Sherronda stepped into her role. Sherronda embraced the shift moving it from a business venture into ministry. She helps to empower, equip, inspire, motivate, and encourage women through various activities and gatherings. Her greatest pursuit out of it all is to see us women healthy, healed, set free, and getting fully delivered from our past or present wounds. She wants to see us as women healed from generational curses, self-inflictions as well as inflictions from others that have caused a halt or stagnation in our lives. Her motto is "If I can just help one person that is good enough for me."

www.ingramcontent.com/pod-product-compliance
Lightning Source LLC
Chambersburg PA
CBHW071411040426
42444CB00009B/2201